THE
PYTHON BIBLE

VOLUME SEVEN
COMPUTER VISION

BY

FLORIAN DEDOV

Copyright © 2020

TABLE OF CONTENT

INTRODUCTION

Computer vision is one of the most exciting and interesting topics in computer science. This field focuses on how computers perceive and process image and video data. The technologies of this area are fundamental for our future, with virtual reality and internet of things becoming more and more important. With computer vision we can make unreadable, fuzzy and poorly lit pictures readable. We can also recognize objects and faces in real-time. And we can apply filters, transformations and numerous awesome effects.

In the programming language Python we can use the library OpenCV (also available for other programming languages), which allows us to see a lot of impressive results, with very few lines of code.

These skills are essential for many applications like surveillance and security systems. The whole field of robotics is largely based on computer vision as well. But also in medicine, image processing, filmmaking, industry and automation, computer vision is very important.

THIS BOOK

In this book you are going to learn, how to make interesting computer vision applications, using Python and OpenCV. Each chapter will start with a little bit of theory, followed by practical examples and applications.

For this book however, you will need some advanced Python skills already and a basic understanding of data science. You should be comfortable using NumPy, Matplotlib and Pandas. If you are not, I recommend reading my data science book (volume three) or learning the material from other sources. We will use some of these libraries in this book, but I am not going to explain their basic workings in detail here.

Also, if you are missing some Python skills, you can take a look at my Amazon author page. There you will find the full Python Bible series which contains two volumes for the basics of Python, followed by volumes about data science, machine learning and financial analysis with Python. Of course you can also learn these things from other sources. However, in this book there won't be any explanations of basic Python syntax or the data science libraries mentioned above.

My Amazon Author Page: https://amzn.to/38yY9cG

HOW TO READ THIS BOOK

Essentially it is up to you how you are going to read this book. If you think that the initial chapters are not interesting to you or that you already know everything, you can skip them. Also you can read the book from cover to cover without ever writing a single line of code yourself. But I don't recommend all of this.

I personally recommend you to read all the chapters in the right order, since they build on top of each other. The code samples also work without the previous chapters but then you will lack the understanding of the material and you will have no clue why something works or not.

Additionally it is tremendously important that you code along while reading. That's the only way you will really understand the topics of this book. There will be a lot of code in the individual chapters. Read through it, understand it but also implement it on your own machine and experiment around. What happens when you tweak individual parameters? What happens when you add something? Try everything!

That's all that needs to be said for now. I wish you a lot of success and fun learning about computer vision in Python. I hope that this book will help you to progress in your programming career.

Just one little thing before we start. This book was written for you, so that you can get as much value as possible and learn to code effectively. If you find this book valuable or you think you have learned something new, please write a quick review on Amazon. It is completely free and takes about one minute. But it helps me produce more high quality books, which you can benefit from.

Thank you!

If you are interested in free educational content about programming and machine learning, check out: https://www.neuralnine.com/

INSTALLING LIBRARIES

For this book we will need a couple of libraries that are not part of the default core stack of Python. This means that we need to install them separately using *pip*.

First of all, we are going to install the data science stack:

```
pip install numpy
```

```
pip install matplotlib
```

```
pip install pandas
```

As mentioned in the introduction, you should be comfortable using these libraries already. They are not the main focus of this book but they are going to help us a lot with certain tasks. The main library that we will need for this book is OpenCV. We also install it using pip:

```
pip install opencv-python
```

All these libraries will do a lot of the work for us that we would otherwise have to do ourselves.

1 – LOADING IMAGES AND VIDEOS

Before we start with the processing of images and videos, we will need to learn how to load the respective data into our script. This is what we are going to learn in this first chapter.

For this chapter we will need the following imports:

```
import cv2 as cv
import matplotlib.pyplot as plt
```

Notice that OpenCV was named *opencv-python* in the installation but in order to use it we import *cv2*. I chose to use the *cv* alias here, so that the code is also compatible with eventual future versions. Also, we import Matplotlib, which is useful when working with images.

LOADING IMAGES

In order to load an image, we first need to prepare one. Here you can just download images from the internet or use your own photos. For this book I will use license-free images from Pixabay or images that I made myself.

```
img = cv.imread('car.jpg', cv.IMREAD_COLOR)
```

To now load the image into our script, we use the *imread* function of OpenCV. First we pass our file path, followed by the color scheme that we want to use.

In this case we choose *IMREAD_COLOR* because we want to work with the colored version of the image. We can now go ahead and show the image.

```
cv.imshow('Car', img)
cv.waitKey(0)
cv.destroyAllWindows()
```

For this we use the *imshow* function, which accepts the title of the images (the identifier) and the image itself. After that you can see two more commands, which we are going to use quite often. The first one is the *waitKey* function, which waits for a key to be pressed, before the script continues. The parameter it takes is the delay. In this case we chose zero. After that, we have the *destroyAllWindows* function, which does what the name says.

Fig. 1.1: Image of a car in OpenCV

If we choose to use the *IMREAD_GRAYSCALE* color scheme, instead of the *IMREAD_COLOR* color scheme, our image would look like this.

Fig. 1.2: Grayscale version of the image

Of course if you are reading a black-and-white version of this book, you will not see a difference. So run the code yourself to see the difference.

SHOWING IMAGES WITH MATPLOTLIB

Another way of showing our images is by using Matplotlib. Here we also have and *imshow* function, which visualizes images.

```
plt.imshow(img)
plt.show()
```

The problem that we will encounter here however is, that Matplotlib uses a different color scheme from the one OpenCV uses. This results in the following image.

Fig. 1.3: Image of a car in Matplotlib

Again if you are reading a non-color version of this book, you might not see the clear difference here. In this case, you need to execute the code.

CONVERTING COLOR SCHEMES

While OpenCV uses the RGB color scheme (red, green, blue), Matplotlib uses the BGR color scheme (blue, green, red). This basically means that the values for blue and red are swapped in our image. In order to change that, we can convert the color scheme.

```
img = cv.cvtColor(img, cv.COLOR_RGB2BGR)
```

By using the *cvtColor* function, we can convert our image. For this we first pass the image itself, followed by the conversion that we want to happen. In this case we choose *COLOR_RGB2BGR*, since we want to convert our image from RGB to BGR. After that we can see the right colors in Matplotlib.

LOADING VIDEOS

Besides images, we can also load videos into our script, using OpenCV.

```
import cv2 as cv

video = cv.VideoCapture('city.mp4')

while True:
    ret, frame = video.read()

    cv.imshow('City Video', frame)

    if cv.waitKey(30) == ord('x'):
        break

video.release()
cv.destroyAllWindows()
```

Here we use the *VideoCapture* object and pass the file path of our video. Then we run an endless loop which constantly reads one frame after the other, using the *read* function. We then show this frame with the *imshow* method. At the end of our loop, we then use the *waitKey* function that checks if the 'x' key was pressed (replacable). If we press it, the script terminates. As a delay we choose 30, which means that we will wait 30 milliseconds before we show the next frame. One second has 1000 milliseconds. When we show one frame every 30 milliseconds, we end up with an FPS rate of 33 frames per second. Of course you can change the values if you want. Last but not least, we then call the *release* function to release our capture. This is like closing a stream.

Fig. 1.4: Screenshot of the video

Now we have one problem. When the video is finished and we don't terminate it manually, our script crashes and we get an error. We can easily fix this with a little if-statement, which checks for return values.

```
while True:
    ret, frame = video.read()
```

```
if ret:
    cv.imshow('City Video', frame)

    if cv.waitKey(30) == ord('x'):
        break
else:
    break
```

Alternatively we can also run the same video over and over again in the loop. This is done by replacing the *break* with a line that resets the video.

```
while True:
    ret, frame = video.read()

    if ret:
        cv.imshow('City Video', frame)

        if cv.waitKey(30) == ord('x'):
            break
    else:
        video = cv.VideoCapture('city.mp4')
```

Now every time the video is finished, it will start all over again.

LOADING CAMERA DATA

Last but not least let us talk about getting our camera data into the script. Instead of specifying a file path in our *VideoCapture* object, we can specify a number (index of the camera), in order to view the data of our camera in real-time.

```
import cv2 as cv

video = cv.VideoCapture(0)

while True:
    ret, frame = video.read()

    if ret:
        cv.imshow('City Video', frame)

        if cv.waitKey(1) == ord('x'):
            break
    else:
        video = cv.VideoCapture('city.mp4')

video.release()
cv.destroyAllWindows()
```

Here we choose zero as the video source, which will be the primary camera. If you have two, three or more cameras, you can change that index, to select those.

We can also tweak the delay of the *waitKey* function, in order to adjust the FPS. If you are installing a camera for surveillance, you might want to choose a lower FPS rate (and thus a higher delay) because the cameras are running 24/7 and you don't want to waste too much disk space. But if you want to play around with some filters or effects, you will choose a delay of around one second.

2 – FUNDAMENTAL EDITING

Now that we know how to load images, videos and camera data, we can start talking about some fundamental editing.

DRAWING

Let's first take a look at how to draw on our images. With OpenCV we can paint simple shapes like lines, rectangles and circles onto our pictures.

```
cv.line(img, (50,50), (250,250), (255,255,0), 15)
cv.rectangle(img, (350,450), (500,350),
(0,255,0), 5)
cv.circle(img, (500, 200), 100, (255,0,0), 7)
```

For this we use the functions *line, rectangle* and *circle*. But of course we also have others like *fillPoly* to fill polygons.

The parameters vary from function to function. To *line* and *rectangle* we pass the two points right after the image in form of a tuple. These are the starting point and the end point. The two values are the x- and the y-coordinates. Then we also pass a triple with the RGB values for the color. Finally, we specify the thickness of the line.

For the circle on the other hand, we first need to specify one point (which is the center) and then the radius. At the end, we again specify the line thickness.

Fig. 2.1: Drawing shapes with OpenCV

In the figure above you can see what this looks like. This primitive drawing is primarily useful when we want to highlight something specific. For example when we want to but a box around a certain object when it is recognized. We are going to do this in a later chapter.

DRAWING WITH MATPLOTLIB

It is also possible to use Matplotlib for our drawings. I am not going to get into the details of Matplotlib plotting here, since I covered it in volume three already. However, let's look at a quick example of plotting a function onto our image.

```
x_values = np.linspace(100,900,50)
y_values = np.sin(x_values) * 100 + 300

plt.imshow(img, cmap='gray')
plt.plot(x_values,y_values, 'c', linewidth=5)
plt.show()
```

Here for example we plot a modified sine function onto our car. Of course this doesn't make any sense in this particular case but there are definitely scenarios in which that might be useful.

Fig. 2.2: Plotting function over the image

COPYING ELEMENTS

What we can also do with OpenCV is to copy or cut certain parts of the image and then use them elsewhere. This is done with index slicing.

```
img[0:200, 0:300] = [0, 0, 0]
```

In this example we replace all the pixels from 0 to 200 on the y-axis and from 0 to 300 on the x-axis with black pixels. We assign a list with three zeros that represent the RGB color codes.

Fig. 2.3: Replaced upper-left corner

With index slicing, as we just used it, we can also move or copy various parts of our image.

```
copypart = img[300:500, 300:700]
```

```
img[100:300, 100:500] = copypart
```

With this code we store all the pixels from 300 to 500 on the y-axis and from 300 to 700 on the x-axis in a temporary variable. Then we assign these values to another part of the image, which has the same resolution.

```
img[300:500, 300:700] = [0,0,0]
```

If you want to move the part, instead of copying it, you should replace the initial pixels with black color. However, be careful with intersections because you might overwrite the part you just moved. It is probably a better idea to first black out the initial part and then paste the copied piece.

Fig. 2.4: Moving and copying of image parts

The difference is obvious. On the one picture we just copied and pasted the section, whereas we replaced it on the other one.

SAVING IMAGES AND VIDEOS

When we are done with the processing of our images and videos, we will want to export them. For images this is quite easy.

```
cv.imwrite('car_new.jpg', img)
```

We just use the *imwrite* method of OpenCV. Depending on the file type we specify, the image will be encoded accordingly.

SAVING VIDEOS

Saving videos is also not really complex. But here we need to define some additional things.

```
capture = cv.VideoCapture(0)
fourcc = cv.VideoWriter_fourcc(*'XVID')
writer = cv.VideoWriter('video.avi', fourcc, 60.0,
(640,480))
```

Besides the *VideoCapture* we also need to specify the so-called *FourCC*. This is the codec that we are going to use to encode the video data and it specifies the format. In this case we pick XVID. This is an open-source variation of the MPEG-4 codec.

Additionally, we also need to define a *VideoWriter*. To this we pass the file name, the codec, the frame rate and the desired resolution. In this case we save our video into the *video.avi* file with 60 FPS and a resolution of 640x480 pixels.

```
while True:
    ret, frame = capture.read()

    writer.write(frame)

    cv.imshow('Cam', frame)

    if cv.waitKey(1) == ord('x'):
        break
```

In our endless loop we then call the *write* function with each iteration, in order to write our frames into the file.

```
capture.release()
writer.release()
cv.destroyAllWindows()
```

Last but not least, we release all the components and
close all windows. That is how we save video data
into a file with OpenCV.

3 – THRESHOLDING

Now we are getting into one of the most interesting topics of computer vision, which is *thresholding*. Here everything is about segmenting our image data. This is important fr technologies like object and face recognition but also for the filtering of information and the optimization of poorly taken images.

INSERT LOGO

In the following section we are going to use thresholding in order to make a logo partly transparent and then insert it into an image.

Fig. 3.1: Image of a workspace

This license-free image is the main background and we want to insert the logo in the upper-left corner.

Fig. 3.2: Sample logo

This will be our sample logo. It is a white M on blue background. What we now want is the M to be transparent, so that we can look through it onto our background. For this we will use thresholding. We will find the white area with OpenCV and then make it transparent.

```
img1 = cv.imread('laptop.jpg')
img2 = cv.imread('logo.png')
```

For this we first load both of the images into our script. In the next step we get to thresholding.

```
logo_gray = cv.cvtColor(img2,
cv.COLOR_RGB2GRAY)
ret, mask = cv.threshold(logo_gray, 180, 255,
cv.THRESH_BINARY_INV)
```

We are converting the logo into the grayscale color scheme because we are only interested in the while color. For this we use the color mode *COLOR_RGB2GRAY*. Then we use the *threshold* function. To it we pass the grayscale logo and also from which color value, we want to change to which color value. In this example, we choose to convert every pixel that has a higher value than 180 (light gray) to 255 (totally white). For this we use the *THRESH_BINARY_INV* procedure.

As one of the return values we get the mask of this image, which we can visualize.

```
cv.imshow('Mask', mask)
```

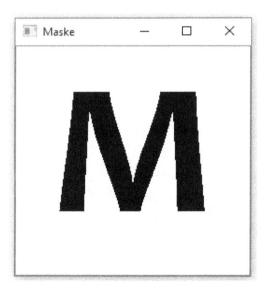

Fig. 3.3: Mask after thresholding

In order to understand the next step here, we first need to understand what we are actually trying to accomplish here. We want to get the blue background unchanged and we want to completely remove the white area. For this we can use the bitwise AND. This is a logical operation, which returns True, when both operands are True. In our context the color black means False and the color white means True. When we perform a logical AND with the white color, we get as a result the other operand, since white accepts everything. So when we apply a logical AND operation to our background and the white color, the result will be the background itself.

With the black color it is the exact opposite. Since this number represents False, the result will be adapted to zero percent and nothing changes.

If you have understood this basic principle, you should recognize what is wrong with our mask. It is the exact opposite of what it should be. We need a white M so that it can become transparent and we need a black background so that it doesn't change. Therefore, we will invert the mask.

```
mask_inv = cv.bitwise_not(mask)
mask_inv = np.invert(mask) # Alternative way
```

Here we can either use the *bitwise_not* function of OpenCV or the *invert* function of NumPy. Just don't use both because then you invert it twice and end up with the original mask.

Now let's get to the actual inserting of the logo. First we need to determine how big this logo is and select the proper region for our AND operation.

```
rows, columns, channels = img2.shape
area = img1[0:rows, 0:columns]
```

We use the *shape* attribute of our logo in order to get the resolution and the channels. Then we save the respective area of our background into a variable.

```
img1_bg = cv.bitwise_and(area, area, mask=mask_inv)
img2_fg = cv.bitwise_and(img2, img2, mask=mask)
```

Now we apply the bitwise operations. We define two parts of the upper-left corner, which we then combine in the end. First we define the background of the initial picture, by applying the inverted mask to the selected area. This makes the M transparent. The second line of code then adds the mask with the blue background.

```
result = cv.add(img1_bg, img2_fg)
img1[0:rows, 0:columns] = result
```

Last but not least, we use the *add* function to combine both layers. Then we assign the result to the upper-left corner of the final image.

```
cv.imshow('Result', img1)
```

Fig. 3.4: Result of the thresholding

The image is now exactly the way we wanted it to be.

MAKING POORLY LIT IMAGES READABLE

Let us now get to an example that is a little bit more impressive than just adding a logo.

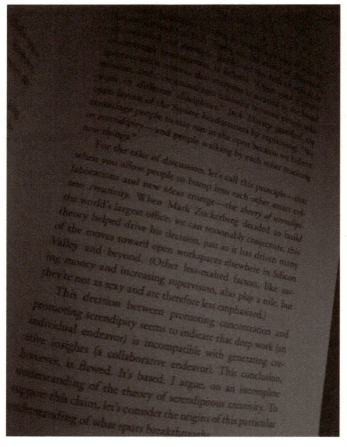

Fig. 3.5: Poorly lit book page

Can you clearly read what is written on that book page? It's not that it's impossible but it is pretty hard. The lighting conditions are pretty bad. With thresholding however, we can fix that problem. We can make that text easily readable.

One first idea would be to just convert the image to grayscale and apply the binary thresholding.

```
img = cv.imread('bookpage.jpg')
img_gray = cv.cvtColor(img, cv.COLOR_RGB2GRAY)
ret, threshold = cv.threshold(img_gray, 32,
255, cv.THRESH_BINARY)
```

Every pixel that is whiter than 32 (dark gray) is now being converted to 255 (completely white) and every value below is converted to 0 (completely black).

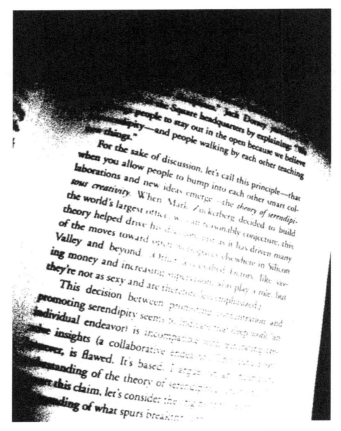

Fig. 3.6: Result after binary thresholding

As you can see the result isn't that good. Parts of the image that we want to be white are black and vice versa. We obviously need a more dynamic way of thresholding.

Here the *adaptive Gaussian thresholding* comes into play. This algorithm allows us the use the binary thresholding more dynamically.

```
gaus = cv.adaptiveThreshold(img_gray, 255,

cv.ADAPTIVE_THRESH_GAUSSIAN_C,
                            cv.THRESH_BINARY, 81, 4)
```

We first pass our gray picture, followed by the maximum value (255 for white). Then we choose the adaptive algorithm which is the Gaussian one in this case (*ADAPTIVE_THRESH_GAUSSIAN_C*). After that we choose the thresholding that we want to use, which is still the binary thresholding. Now the last two parameters are essential. The first one is the block size and specifies how large (in pixels) the blocks used for thresholding shall be. The larger this value is, the more will be taken into the calculations. Smaller details might not be valued as that important then. This value needs to be odd and for this case 81 is a good choice. The last parameter is called *C* and it specifies how much shall be subtracted from the median value. With this parameter we oftentimes need to experiment a little bit. It sharpens and smooths the image.

```
cv.imshow('Gaus', gaus)
```

Now let us look at our final result.

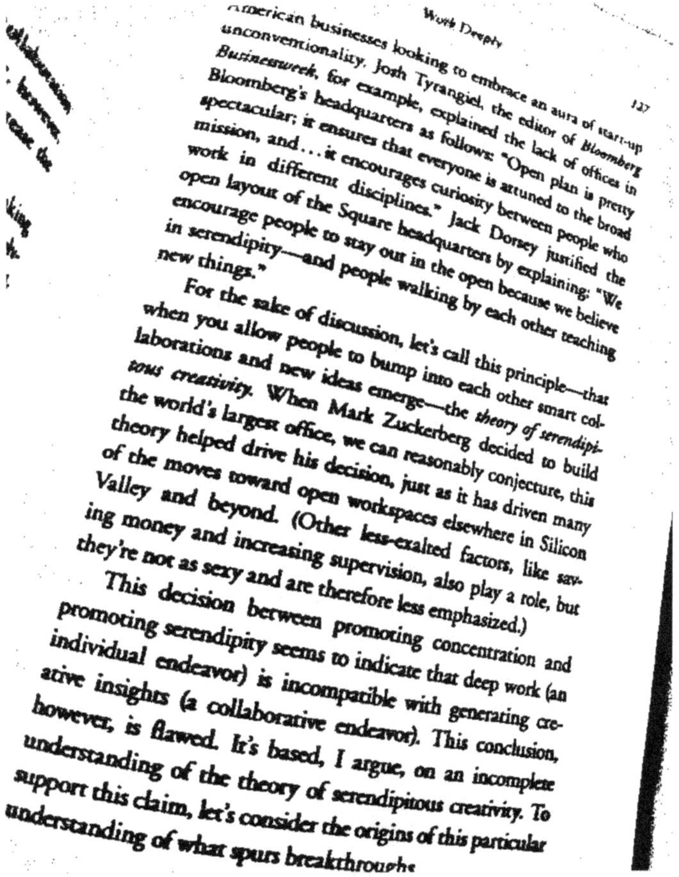

American businesses looking to embrace an aura of start-up unconventionality, Josh Tyrangiel, the editor of *Bloomberg Businessweek*, for example, explained the lack of offices in Bloomberg's headquarters as follows: "Open plan is pretty spectacular; it ensures that everyone is attuned to the broad mission, and... it encourages curiosity between people who work in different disciplines." Jack Dorsey justified the open layout of the Square headquarters by explaining: "We encourage people to stay out in the open because we believe in serendipity—and people walking by each other teaching new things."

For the sake of discussion, let's call this principle—that when you allow people to bump into each other, smart collaborations and new ideas emerge—the *theory of serendipitous creativity*. When Mark Zuckerberg decided to build the world's largest office, we can reasonably conjecture, this theory helped drive his decision, just as it has driven many of the moves toward open workspaces elsewhere in Silicon Valley and beyond. (Other less-exalted factors, like saving money and increasing supervision, also play a role, but they're not as sexy and are therefore less emphasized.)

This decision between promoting concentration and promoting serendipity seems to indicate that deep work (an individual endeavor) is incompatible with generating creative insights (a collaborative endeavor). This conclusion, however, is flawed. It's based, I argue, on an incomplete understanding of the theory of serendipitous creativity. To support this claim, let's consider the origins of this particular understanding of what spurs breakthroughs

Fig. 3.6: Results after adaptive thresholding

This result is actually quite impressive. It is not perfect but we can easily read the whole text without any problems.

By the way the book page that you see here is from the book *Deep Work* from *Cal Newport*.

As you can see many things are possible with thresholding. Before you continue with the next chapter, try to apply what you have just learned onto your own images. Maybe you could make some poorly lit images or come up with new creative ideas for the application of thresholding. Experiment a little bit and play around with these technologies.

4 – FILTERING

In this chapter we are going to talk about *filtering*. However we are not talking about the filters that people use on social media to make their pictures prettier. We are talking about actually filtering specific information out of pictures.

For example we might want to extract all the red objects from a video or an image. Or we might be interested in those parts that are brighter than a specific limit.

Fig. 4.1: Image of a parrot

Let's use this simple image as our example. Here we have a red parrot in front of a blue-green background. With filtering algorithms we can now try to extract and highlight the feathers.

This might be useful for a number of reasons. You might want to recognize specific object or patterns. This particular example is trivial but it will illustrate the concept.

CREATING A FILTER MASK

The first step is to now load our image into the script. At the end of this chapter, we are also going to talk about filtering videos and camera data.

```
img = cv.imread('parrot.jpg')
hsv = cv.cvtColor(img, cv.COLOR_RGB2HSV)
```

What's important here is that we won't work with the RGB color scheme. We are going to convert it into HSV. RGB stands for *Red, Green, Blue*, whereas HSV stands for *Hue, Saturation, Value*.

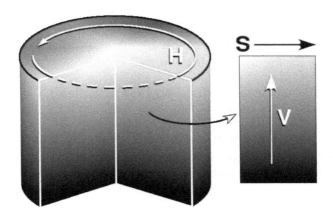

Fig. 4.2: HSV color scheme (Source: Wikipedia)

The H-value determines the color we are choosing from the spectrum. The S-value indicates how high our saturation is or how "strong" the colors are. And the V-value states how bright the chosen color shall be.

We are choosing this color scheme because it is much easier to filter images, using these three parameters.

```
minimum = np.array([100, 60, 0])
maximum = np.array([255, 255, 255])
```

This takes us to the next step. Now we are going to define two limits or boundaries – the minimum and the maximum. The color value than has to be in between of those, in order to be extracted. In our case, the color value has to be in between 100 and 255. This gives us all values that represent orange or red colors. Also we demand a saturation of at least 60, in order to not get any gray values. For this example we will ignore the brightness and therefore allow for the full spectrum from 0 to 255.

```
mask = cv.inRange(hsv, minimum, maximum)
result = cv.bitwise_and(img, img, mask = mask)
```

Next we are going to define a mask by using the *inRange* function. This function sets all pixels that match our requirements to white pixels and all the others to black pixels. Then we use the logical *bitwise_and* function, in order to AND the original image with itself and apply the mask.

```
cv.imshow('Mask', mask)
```

Let's take a quick look at the mask we created.

Fig. 4.3: Resulting filter mask

The white pixels are the ones that we are extracting for our result. For this, we will look at the actual result.

```
cv.imshow('Result', result)
```

Fig. 4.4: Resulting image

Actually, that is a quite a nice result already. But we can still see individual pixels that shouldn't be there. Especially when you are filtering camera data in real-time you will notice a lot of background noise.

BLURRING AND SMOOTHING

To now optimize the result we will use *blurring* and *smoothing*. We are going to make our result less sharp but also reduce the background noise and the unwanted pixels. The first step for this is to create an array for the averages.

```
averages = np.ones((15, 15), np.float32) / 225
```

Here we create an array full of ones that has the shape 15x15. We then divide this array by 225 (the product of 15x15). Then we end up with a factor for each pixel that calculates the average.

The goal here is to correct individual unwanted pixels by looking at the average pixels in 15x15 pixel fields.

```
smoothed = cv.filter2D(result, -1, averages)
```

With the *filter2D* function we apply this averages kernel onto our image. The second parameter, which is set to -1, specifies the depth of the image. Since we choose a negative value, we just copy the depth of the original image.

```
cv.imshow('Smoothed', smoothed)
```

Fig. 4.5: Resulting smoothed image

As you can see, most of the unwanted pixels are gone. But the picture is now pretty blurry.

Notice that the order of these steps is very relevant. Here we first applied the mask onto our image and then smoothed the result. We could also do it the other way around and first make the mask smoother. Then we get a different result.

```
smoothed2 = cv.filter2D(mask, -1, averages)
smoothed2 = cv.bitwise_and(img, img,
mask=smoothed2)

cv.imshow('Smoothed2', smoothed2)
```

Fig. 4.6: Resulting image after smoothing the mask

In this particular example, the second order is useless. We have many more unwanted pixels than before the smoothing. However, this will be useful with other algorithms.

Gaussian Blur

Another method which we could apply here is the Gaussian blur.

```
blur = cv.GaussianBlur(result, (15, 15), 0)
```

Here we also pass the size of the blocks to blur. The result is a little bit less blurry than the previous one.

Median Blur

The probably most effective blur is the *median blur*. This one processes each channel of an image individually and applies the median filter.

```
median = cv.medianBlur(result, 15)

cv.imshow('Median', median)
```

Here we only pass the image and the block size which is quadratic. In this case we again have 15x15 pixels.

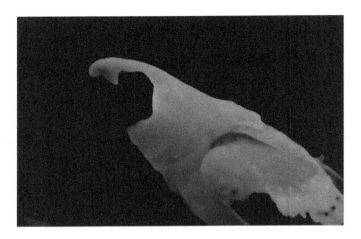

Fig. 4.7: Resulting image after median blur

This result is definitely impressive, since there is no background noise left. However, we can do even better. As you can see the image is still pretty blurry and this can be changed by changing the order of the methods.

```
median2 = cv.medianBlur(mask, 15)
median2 = cv.bitwise_and(img, img,
mask=median2)

cv.imshow('Median2', median2)
```

Fig. 4.8: Result after changing the order

This is by far the best result. We don't have any unwanted pixels and the picture is not blurry at all. For this particular example, the median blur turns out to be the best choice.

FILTERING CAMERA DATA

As I already mentioned, what we just did with the parrot image we can also do with the camera data in real time.

```python
import cv2 as cv
import numpy as np

camera = cv.VideoCapture(0)

while True:
    _, img = camera.read()
    hsv = cv.cvtColor(img, cv.COLOR_RGB2HSV)
```

```
    minimum = np.array([100, 60, 0])
    maximum = np.array([255, 255, 255])

    mask = cv.inRange(hsv, minimum, maximum)

    median = cv.medianBlur(mask, 15)
    median = cv.bitwise_and(img, img,
mask=median)

    cv.imshow('Median', median)

    if cv.waitKey(5) == ord('x'):
        break

cv.destroyAllWindows()
camera.release()
```

Again we just create a capturing object and read the frames in an endless loop. Then, in every iteration, we applied the filter on the frame before actually showing it. If you try this at home with your own camera, you will notice that everything that is not red or orange will be invisible.

As always, I encourage you to play around with these filters yourself. Change the HSV settings. Use different images. Tweak all the parameters. Learn how the filters work and which are the most effective for different scenarios.

5 – OBJECT RECOGNITION

Now we get into one of the most interesting subfields of computer vision, which is *object recognition*. In the beginning of this chapter we are going to cover topics like *edge detection*, *template and feature matching* and *background subtraction*. At the end we will then use cascading to recognize actual objects in images and videos.

EDGE DETECTION

Let's start talking about edge detection. Oftentimes it is quite useful to reduce our images and videos to the most essential information. In this book we are not going to write our own object recognition algorithms from scratch. But if we wanted to do it, detecting edges would be a very useful tool.

Fig. 5.1: Image of a room

For this example we will use this image of an ordinary room. A computer is not really interested in details like shadows and lighting. Therefore we are going to use an algorithm, in order to filter out the essential edges.

```python
import cv2 as cv

img = cv.imread('room.jpg')
edges = cv.Canny(img, 100, 100)
cv.imshow('Edges', edges)

cv.waitKey(0)
cv.destroyAllWindows()
```

The *Canny* function of OpenCV does this for us. We pass the original image followed by two tolerance values. The result looks quite interesting.

Fig. 5.2: Image after edge detection

As you can see, all the essential information is still there but the image was reduced to its edges.

TEMPLATE MATCHING

Another interesting technique is *template matching*. Here we give our script some templates for specific objects, which it then has to find in the images. The difference to object recognition however is that the matching has to be pretty accurate. It is looking for almost exact matches rather than similar patterns. Thus, this technique is not optimal for the general recognition of faces or clocks for example.

Fig. 5.3: Image of a workspace

Let's take this image of a workspace as our example. Basically, we could choose any object we want, but the only one that occurs multiple times in this image are they keys of the laptop keyboard.

Fig 5.4: F-key as template

So what we do is we crop out one of the keys using a program like Gimp or Photoshop. Then we use this key as our template image.

```
img_bgr = cv.imread('workspace.jpg')
img_gray = cv.cvtColor(img_bgr,
cv.COLOR_BGR2GRAY)

template = cv.imread('key.jpg', 0)
width, height = template.shape[::-1]
```

First we load the main picture and the template into our program. Then we make a copy of the image and convert it into grayscale. Also we save the width and the height of the template in pixels.

```
result = cv.matchTemplate(img_gray, template,

cv.TM_CCOEFF_NORMED)
```

The main work will now be done by the *matchTemplate* function. To it we pass our image, our template and we specify the method that we are going to use for matching. In this case *TM_CCOEFF_NORMED*.

What we get as a result is an array with the respective activations of the image parts, in which this template occurs.

```
threshold = 0.8
area = np.where(result >= threshold)
```

In the next step we define a certain threshold. It specifies how far the pixels of the grayscale image are allowed to deviate from the template. In this case 0.8 means that the area needs to have at least 80% similarity with our template to be recognized as a match. You can tweak this value as you like and experiment around. The function *where* from NumPy returns the indices of the pixels, which are close enough.

```
for pixel in zip(*area[::-1]):
    cv.rectangle(img_bgr, pixel,
                (pixel[0] + width, pixel[1] +
height),
                (0, 0, 255), 2)
```

Now we run a for loop over the zipped version of our area. For each pixel in this area, which has a high enough activation, we will then draw a red rectangle of the width and height of the template. This will then indicate that our algorithm has found a match there.

```
cv.imshow('Result', img_bgr)
cv.waitKey(0)
cv.destroyAllWindows()
```

Last but not least, we can look at our result with all the matches.

Fig. 5.5: Workspace after feature matching

Again, if you are reading a grayscale version of this book, you will probably only notice the gray rectangles around some of the keys. When you execute the script yourself, you will see that they are red.

As you can see, our algorithm recognized quite a lot of keys. If you want to find more keys, you will have to reduce the threshold. In this case however, you also increase the likelihood of misclassifications.

FEATURE MATCHING

Imagine having two pictures that show the exact same objects but from a different perspective.

Fig. 5.6: Workspace from another perspective

Here for example we have the workspace from a different perspective. For us humans it is not hard to recognize that these objects are the same and match them in both pictures. But for our computer these are completely different pixels.

What's going to help us here is the so-called *feature matching*. Here, algorithms extract all the essential points and descriptors of our images. Then it looks for the same points in the other image and connects them.

```
img1 = cv.imread('workspace1.jpg', 0)
img2 = cv.imread('workspace2.jpg', 0)

orb = cv.ORB_create()

keypoints1, descriptors1 =
orb.detectAndCompute(img1, None)
```

```
keypoints2, descriptors2 =
orb.detectAndCompute(img2, None)
```

After loading our images, we create an *orientational BRIEF* (short ORB). This will help us to determine the essential points. We call the *detectAndCompute* function of this object and apply it to both our images. The results we get are the key points and the descriptors for both images.

In this example, we import the images in black and white (thus the zero). We do this because we can then better see the colored connections in the end. But you can also load the original images if you want.

```
matcher = cv.BFMatcher(cv.NORM_HAMMING,
crossCheck=True)
matches = matcher.match(descriptors1, descriptors2)
matches = sorted(matches, key = lambda x:
x.distance)
```

Now we create an instance of the *BFMatcher* class and choose the *NORM_HAMMING* algorithm. This matcher allows us to combine the key points and determine where the key points of one picture can be found in the other one. The result will then be sorted by distance in the last line, so that we have the shortest distances first. This is important because in the next step we are only going to filter out a couple of the best results.

```
result = cv.drawMatches(img1,keypoints1,
                        img2,keypoints2,
                        matches[:10], None, flags=2)
```

Last but not least, we visualize these matches with the *drawMatches* function. For this we pass both images, their key points and specify which matches shall be visualized. In this case we pick the first ten matches, which have the shortest distance.

```
result = cv.resize(result, (1600,900))
cv.imshow('Result',result)
cv.waitKey(0)
```

Now we scale the final result so that we can show the images without problems.

Fig. 5.7: Feature matching of both images

It is very hard to actually see the lines in this book. Even if you have a colored version, you will struggle because OpenCV draws very thin lines here. Therefore, go ahead and execute the code on your own machine to see the results.

Basically what is happening is that the most important points in the left image are being connected to the most important points in the right image. This works pretty well most of the time but we still have some mistakes in our result. It's not perfect!

MOVEMENT DETECTION

Before we finally get to object recognition we will take a look at a very interesting technique when it comes to movement detection. This technique is called *background subtraction*. Here we use an algorithm that looks at the changes in pixels, in order to determine what the background is. Then we only focus on the foreground or at those pixels that are changing or moving.

Fig. 5.8: Screenshot of a video

For this I will use a video in which many people are walking at a public place. Of course you can use your own videos or even the camera data as input.

```
# Alternative: video = cv.VideoCapture(0)
video = cv.VideoCapture('people.mp4')
subtractor =
cv.createBackgroundSubtractorMOG2(20, 50)
```

As always we load our video into our script. Then we create a new subtractor by using the function *createBackgroundSubtractorMOG2*. To it we (optionally) pass two parameters. The first one is the length of the *history*, which specifies how far back our subtractor shall look for movements or changes. The second one is the *threshold*. Here again you have to play around with those values until you get optimal results.

```
while True:
    _, frame = video.read()
    mask = subtractor.apply(frame)

    cv.imshow('Mask', mask)

    if cv.waitKey(5) == ord('x'):
        break

cv.destroyAllWindows()
video.release()
```

Now we can once again run our endless loop and show our results. The only thing that we do here is to *apply* our subtractor to the current frame. The result is our mask.

Fig. 5.9: Result as mask

Even though the result is not perfect and we can probably choose better parameters, the subtractor fulfills its purpose. We can only see those parts of the video that are changing. This is the foreground. Try it yourself. It is fun!

OBJECT RECOGNITION

Now we finally get to *object recognition*. Here we try to work as generalized as possible. This is the opposite strategy of template matching. Our goal is not to find the same type of key or the same face but to generally recognize faces, computers, keys etc. For this however, we need some advanced models and training data. Since it takes quite a lot of effort to build those on our own, we will use resources from the internet.

LOADING RESSOURCES

We will make use of so-called *HaarCascades*, which have the format of XML files. In this book we are going to use one of these cascades for recognizing faces and one of them to recognize clocks. For this, we will use the following links:

Face Cascade: https://bit.ly/3bkHNHs

Clock Cascade: https://bit.ly/3bdLQF8

If for some reason the links don't work in the future, you can just look up some *HaarCascades* for the objects that you want to recognize.

However, take care of the licensing of these files. The first file is from the company Intel and has a copyright. As long as you use it for your private learning, this should not be a problem though.

```
faces_cascade =
cv.CascadeClassifier('haarcascade_frontalface_default.x
ml')
clock_cascade = cv.CascadeClassifier('clock.xml')
```

We now create two *CascadeClassifiers* for both objects and pass both XML-files as parameters.

Recognizing Objects

Fig. 5.10: Group of people

First we are going to use this picture of people in order to recognize some faces.

```
img = cv.imread('people.jpg')
img = cv.resize(img, (1400, 900))

gray = cv.cvtColor(img, cv.COLOR_RGB2GRAY)
faces = faces_cascade.detectMultiScale(gray, 1.3, 5)
```

We scale the image and convert it into grayscale. Then we use the *detectMultiScale* function of our classifier, in order to recognize faces with the help of our XML-file. Here we pass two optional parameters. First the scaling factor of the image which is going to be higher the better our image quality is. And second the minimum amount of neighbor classification for a match. That's actually it. We now just have to visualize everything.

```
for (x,y,w,h) in faces:
    cv.rectangle(img, (x, y),
                 (x + w, y + h),
                 (255, 0, 0), 2)
    cv.putText(img, 'FACE',
               (x,y+h+30),
               cv.FONT_HERSHEY_SIMPLEX, 0.8,
               (255,255,255), 2)
```

We iterate over each recognized face and get the two coordinates, the width and the height. Then we draw a rectangle and put a text below it.

Fig. 5.11: Classified faces

As you can see, the result is pretty amazing. We will now do the same thing with clocks.

Fig. 5.12: Image of a room with a clock

In this room you can see a clock, which we want to recognize with our script. We repeat the procedure and add some parts to our script.

In diesem Zimmer befindet sich eine Wanduhr, welche wir von unserem Skript erkennen lassen möchten. Wir wiederholen also die Vorgehensweise und fügen Teile zu unserem Skript hinzu.

```
faces = faces_cascade.detectMultiScale(grau, 1.3, 5)
clock = clock_cascade.detectMultiScale(grau, 1.3, 10)
```

For the clock we use ten as the third parameter, because otherwise it makes some misclassifications.

```
for (x,y,w,h) in clocks:
    cv.rectangle(img, (x, y),
                 (x + w, y + h),
                 (0, 0, 255), 2)
    cv.putText(img, 'CLOCK',
               (x, y + h + 30),
               cv.FONT_HERSHEY_SIMPLEX, 0.8,
               (255, 255, 255), 2)
```

Here we also draw a rectangle and put a text below the clocks. Of course we need to also change the file path of the image that we are loading in the beginning.

Fig. 5.12: Classified clock

As you can see this also works pretty well. Unfortunately I was not able to find a license-free picture with people and clocks on the wall at the same time. However, in such a case our script would recognize both and draw rectangle with different colors and different texts on the right places. This also works with videos and with camera data.

As always experiment around with the concepts you have learned about in this chapter. Use different images, try different cascades and work with your camera. Be creative and try new things because that is how you learn.

WHAT'S NEXT?

If you have understood the concepts in this book and you learned how to apply them, you have made a huge step towards becoming a master programmer and computer scientist. The skills you learned are invaluable in today's economy but also in the future.

You are able to process image and video data in a very complex way and extract important information. In combination with machine learning and data science, this is a very powerful tool.

Depending on the application field, you will need to learn some extra skills, since no book in the whole world could teach you everything. If you go into natural sciences, you will need to learn the respective skills there. It's the same for medicine, for sports and for every other field. Computer science and mathematics alone are not going to get you very far, unless you go into theoretical research. However, you should now have a solid basis in programming and computer science, so that you continue to progress further on your journey. If you choose to build surveillance systems, analyze medical data or do something completely different, is up to you.

If you are interested in more machine learning, take a look at my Amazon author page. There you can find the other volumes of that series that are about machine learning, data science and neural networks.

NEURALNINE

One place where you can get a ton of additional free resources is *NeuralNine*. This is my brand and it has not only books but also a website, a YouTube channel, a blog, an Instagram page and more. On YouTube you can find high quality video tutorials for free. If you prefer text, you might check out my blog for free information. The *@neuralnine* Instagram page is more about infographics, updates and memes. Feel free to check these out!

YouTube: https://bit.ly/3a5KD2i

Website: https://www.neuralnine.com/

Instagram: https://www.instagram.com/neuralnine/

Books: https://www.neuralnine.com/books/

Can't wait to see you there! ☺

Last but not least, a little reminder. This book was written for you, so that you can get as much value as possible and learn to code effectively. If you find this book valuable or you think you learned something new, please write a quick review on Amazon. It is completely free and takes about one minute. But it helps me produce more high quality books, which you can benefit from.

Thank you!

NeuralNine

If you are interested in free educational content about programming and machine learning, check out https://www.neuralnine.com/

There we have free blog posts, videos and more for you! Also, you can follow the ***@neuralnine*** Instagram account for daily infographics and memes about programming and AI!

Website: https://www.neuralnine.com/

Instagram: @neuralnine

YouTube: NeuralNine

Books: https://www.neuralnine.com/books/

www.ingramcontent.com/pod-product-compliance
Lightning Source LLC
LaVergne TN
LVHW092031060326
832903LV00058B/507